DINOSAURS RULED!

DIPLODOCUS

LEIGH ROCKWOOD

PowerKiDS
press™
New York

Published in 2012 by The Rosen Publishing Group, Inc.
29 East 21st Street, New York, NY 10010

First Edition

Editor: Joanne Randolph
Book Design: Kate Laczynski

Photo Credits: Cover, title page by Brian Garvey; cover background (palm tree leaves) © www.iStockphoto.com/dra_schwartz; cover background (palm tree trunk) iStockphoto/Thinkstock; cover background (ginkgo leaves) Hemera/Thinkstock; cover background (fern leaves) Brand X Pictures/Thinkstock; cover background (moss texture) © www.iStockphoto.com/Robert Linton; pp. 4–5, 6, 10 (top left),10–11, 12, 13, 14–15, 16, 17, 18–19, 20–21 © 2011 Orpheus Books Ltd.; p. 7 © www.iStockphoto.com/Anders Aagesen; p. 8 Hemera/Thinkstock; p. 9 Jupiterimages/Comstock/Thinkstock; p. 10 (top right) iStockphoto/Thinkstock; p. 2? Gotor Producciones/Cover/Getty Images.

Library of Congress Cataloging-in-Publication Data

Rockwood, Leigh.
 Diplodocus / by Leigh Rockwood. — 1st ed.
    p. cm. — (Dinosaurs ruled!)
 Includes index.
 ISBN 978-1-4488-4966-6 (library binding) — ISBN 978-1-4488-5082-2 (pbk.) — ISBN 978-1-4488-5083-9 (6-pack)
 1. Diplodocus—Juvenile literature. I. Title.
 QE862.S3R5554 2012
 567.913—dc22
                                        2010050487

Manufactured in the United States of America

CPSIA Compliance Information: Batch #WS11PK: For Further Information contact Rosen Publishing, New York, New York at 1-800-237-9932

CONTENTS

MEET THE DIPLODOCUS

At first glance, the diplodocus might look like it is all neck and tail sitting on four chunky legs. It is no surprise that this dinosaur was one of the longest land animals that ever lived. "Diplodocus" means "double-beamed lizard." A beam is something that gives support in a building. The beams that the

The diplodocus had extra bones beneath its backbone that were shaped like anvils. These are thought to have given extra support for its long neck and tail.

Diplodocus

diplodocus is named for are the supportive bones in its long body.

Paleontologists have learned a lot about the diplodocus by studying its **fossils**. As they study these remains, paleontologists come up with theories, or ideas, about animals that became **extinct** millions of years ago.

THE LATE JURASSIC PERIOD

Geologic time is a system paleontologists use to put Earth's long history into a timeline. The diplodocus lived during the Late Jurassic period, which lasted from about 160 to 145 million years ago. During this period, there were two main continents on Earth. They

There were bony fishes, marine reptiles, dinosaurs, mammal-like animals, and more living during the Late Jurassic period.

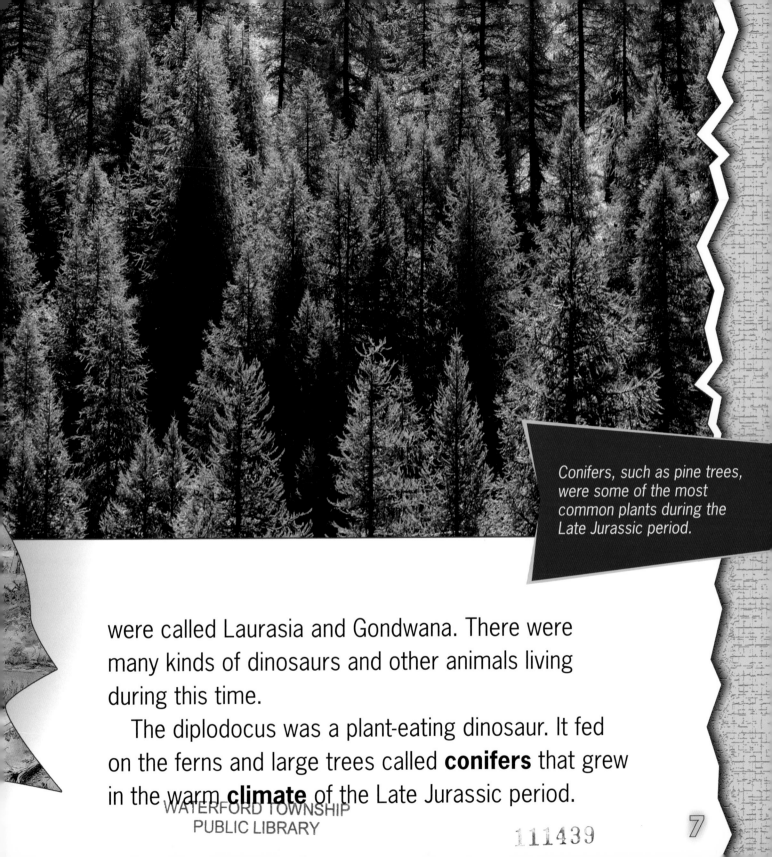

Conifers, such as pine trees, were some of the most common plants during the Late Jurassic period.

were called Laurasia and Gondwana. There were many kinds of dinosaurs and other animals living during this time.

The diplodocus was a plant-eating dinosaur. It fed on the ferns and large trees called **conifers** that grew in the warm **climate** of the Late Jurassic period.

WHERE DID THE DIPLODOCUS LIVE?

Fossils form in **sedimentary rocks**. Sedimentary rocks are made up of layers of sand, mud, and stones that have been pressed together for millions of years. Dead plants and animals sometimes get trapped in these layers of sediment. When this happens, they can become fossilized.

Here you can see the fossilized bones of the head and part of the spine of a diplodocus skeleton.

Many dinosaur fossils, including those of diplodocuses, have been found in the sedimentary rock layers of the Rocky Mountains.

North America has a greater variety of dinosaur fossils than any other place on Earth. Diplodocus fossils have been found in western North America. Many have been found in the Rocky Mountain states of Wyoming, Montana, Colorado, and Utah.

THE DIPLODOCUS'S BODY

The diplodocus had a small head for its body size. Its skull was about as big as a horse's skull is.

The diplodocus is one of the longest dinosaurs that ever lived. A full-grown adult could be up to 90 feet (27 m) long and 16 feet (5 m) tall at the hips. It had a long, whiplike tail. It also had a long neck and a small head.

Although the diplodocus was huge, it was very lightly built for its size. Adults likely weighed between 10 and 20 tons (9–18 t). That is pretty heavy, but the diplodocus was two to three times lighter than other dinosaurs its size.

A diplodocus was longer than two school buses or three African elephants standing end to end. Now picture an animal that big with a head the size of a horse!

NECK AND TAIL

You might think that with a 26-foot-(8 m) long neck, the diplodocus could have easily munched on leaves from high branches. Paleontologists once thought this, too. Today they think that the dinosaur could not reach anything much higher than its shoulders. The latest theory is that the diplodocus reached out and to the sides to nibble on plants.

The diplodocus's body would have been too big for it to walk freely in a forest. Its long neck may have let it reach into forests to find more leaves.

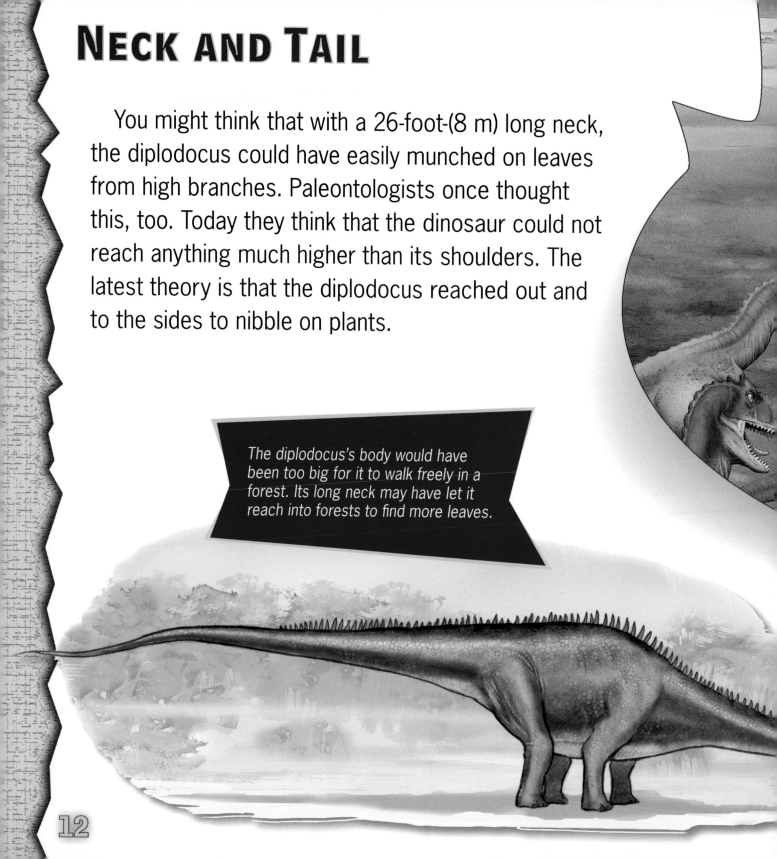

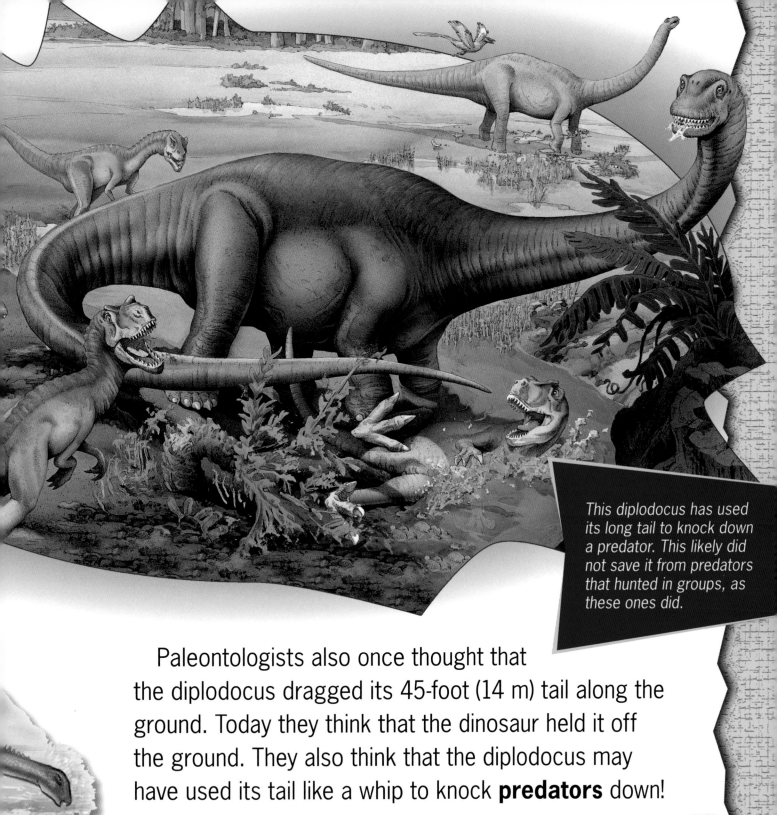

This diplodocus has used its long tail to knock down a predator. This likely did not save it from predators that hunted in groups, as these ones did.

Paleontologists also once thought that the diplodocus dragged its 45-foot (14 m) tail along the ground. Today they think that the dinosaur held it off the ground. They also think that the diplodocus may have used its tail like a whip to knock **predators** down!

TINY BRAIN, BIG FEET

Although it had a big body, the diplodocus had a small head with a tiny brain. Among fellow dinosaurs, the diplodocus would have been one of the least intelligent.

The diplodocus had big feet to carry its large body. Its feet were well padded, with tough skin. They might remind you of an elephant's feet. On each foot there was a claw, which the diplodocus might have used to defend itself. You might think that the diplodocus had a flat-footed walk. Fossils of its footprints show that it walked on its toes, though!

You can see that the diplodocus was larger than many of the other dinosaurs around it. You can also see that its head was much smaller than many other dinosaurs' were.

DINO BITE

Large dinosaurs had thickly padded feet to keep their foot bones from breaking or being hurt while they walked.

15

A Plant-Eating Dinosaur

The diplodocus was an **herbivore**, or plant eater. There were many plants to choose from in the warm, wet **habitat** in which the dinosaur lived. The diplodocus would likely have eaten ferns, club mosses, and horsetails that grew near lakes, rivers, and swamps. Its long neck might have let it stand on dry

The diplodocus would have needed to eat huge amounts of plants to give its body energy.

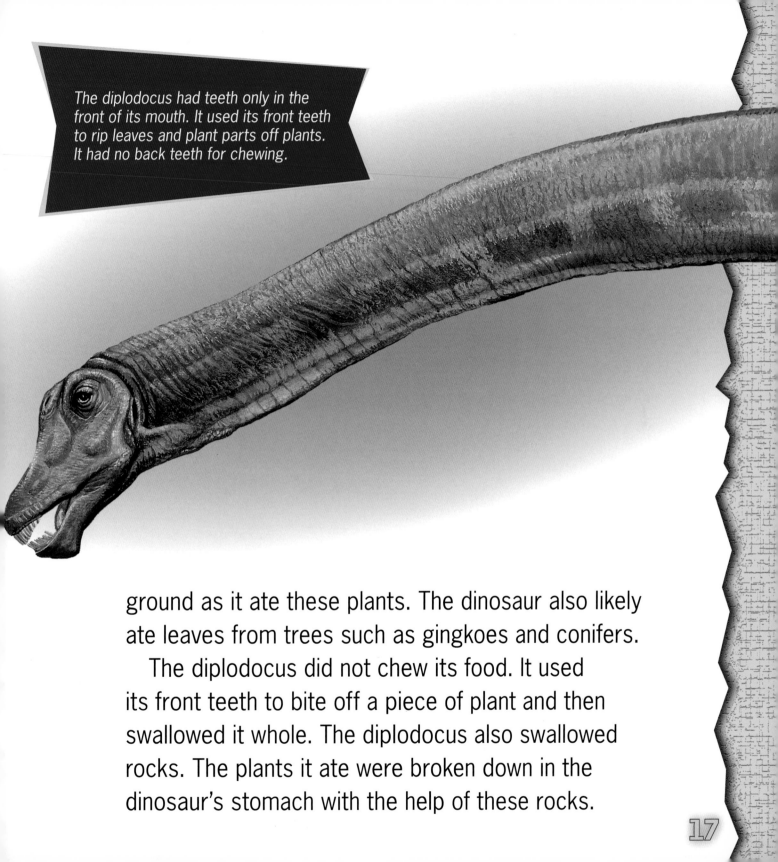

The diplodocus had teeth only in the front of its mouth. It used its front teeth to rip leaves and plant parts off plants. It had no back teeth for chewing.

ground as it ate these plants. The dinosaur also likely ate leaves from trees such as gingkoes and conifers.

The diplodocus did not chew its food. It used its front teeth to bite off a piece of plant and then swallowed it whole. The diplodocus also swallowed rocks. The plants it ate were broken down in the dinosaur's stomach with the help of these rocks.

In the Herd

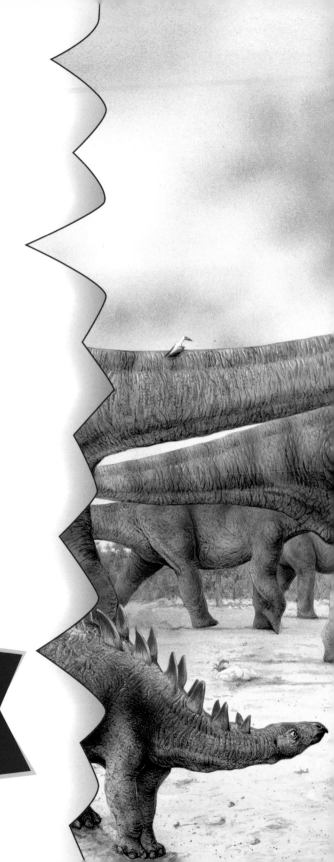

Paleontologists think that diplodocuses traveled in herds. They came to this theory based on some clues they have found. They have found many fossils of diplodocuses in the same place. They have also found lots of diplodocus footprints moving in the same direction. They call the footprint trails dinosaurs leave behind trackways.

Paleontologists think that plant-eating dinosaurs, such as the diplodocus and its relatives, traveled in herds. Many plant eaters today, such as cows, gazelles, and zebras, do this, too.

They use this data and what we know about animals today to guess how the diplodocus might have lived. The dinosaurs likely grazed in groups. They would move on when they had eaten most of the plants in an area.

Lonely Eggs

Like other dinosaurs, diplodocus young **hatched** from eggs. While some dinosaurs kept their eggs in nests and tended to their young, the diplodocus likely did not.

The fossilized eggs of many other dinosaurs have been found grouped in what seem to have been nests. This suggests that those dinosaurs looked after their eggs. Paleontologists have found lines of fossilized diplodocus eggs. What that suggests is that diplodocus mothers laid their eggs and kept on walking! It sounds like a tough start to life, but the diplodocus may have had a life span of around 100 years.

The diplodocus did not look after its eggs. Some of its dinosaur relatives did look after their eggs, though. For example, the mamenchisaurus laid its eggs in a nest and guarded them.

No Bones About It

Earl Douglass and Samuel Williston found the first diplodocus fossil in Colorado in 1877. Paleontologist Othniel Marsh gave the dinosaur its name the next year. Many more diplodocus fossils have been found since then. In fact, the diplodocus is one of the dinosaurs most commonly found in **exhibits** in museums.

This diplodocus skeleton is on exhibit in a museum in Madrid, Spain.

Today paleontologists make computer models of dinosaur fossils before they put the skeleton together. This helps them figure out how the dinosaur likely moved. They want the museum exhibit to look as realistic as possible. Every new fossil that is found adds to the always-growing body of knowledge about dinosaurs.

GLOSSARY

climate (KLY-mit) The kind of weather a certain place has.

conifers (KAH-nih-furz) Trees that have needlelike leaves and grow cones.

exhibits (ig-ZIH-bits) Public shows.

extinct (ik-STINGKT) No longer existing.

fossils (FO-sulz) The hardened remains of dead animals or plants.

habitat (HA-buh-tat) The kind of land where an animal or a plant naturally lives.

hatched (HACHD) Came out of an egg.

herbivore (ER-buh-vor) An animal that eats only plants.

paleontologists (pay-lee-on-TAH-luh-jists) People who study things that lived in the past.

predators (PREH-duh-terz) Animals that kill other animals for food.

sedimentary rocks (seh-deh-MEN-teh-ree ROKS) Stones, sand, or mud that has been pressed together to form rock.

INDEX

WEB SITES

Due to the changing nature of Internet links, PowerKids Press has developed an online list of Web sites related to the subject of this book. This site is updated regularly. Please use this link to access the list:
www.powerkidslinks.com/dinr/diplo/